Be An Expert!

MW01051223

Puppies

Erin Kelly

Children's Press®
An imprint of Scholastic Inc.

Contents

Know the Names

Be an expert! Get to know the names of these puppies.

Retrievers

They are friendly.
They love to play with kids.

Labrador
retrievers

Zoom In

Find these parts in the big picture.

ear

tail

whiskers

paw

golden retrievers

Poodles

They come in three sizes.
They are all really smart.

1 standard poodle

Fetch the Answer

Q: How do you care for a poodle's hair?

A: You need to trim it. A poodle's hair grows long like our hair does. But a poodle doesn't **shed**!

2 miniature poodle

3 toy poodle

Beagles

Throw them a ball.
They love to chase!

Expert Fact

Beagles often **bark** loudly.
They do it to get your attention.

Pointers

They like to run.
Give them lots of space!

German shorthaired
pointer

Expert Fact

Some pointers are great swimmers. They have **webbed** feet like a duck. This helps them pull their bodies through the water.

Hungarian pointer

Terriers

They have so much energy.
Some jump 5 feet in the air!

Boston terriers

Yorkshire terrier

Fetch the Answer

Q: How do you take care of a terrier?

A: Give them lots of exercise! They behave better when you keep them busy.

wire fox terrier

Jack Russell terriers

Bulldogs

They are calm.
They are gentle with kids.

English
bulldogs

Find these parts in the big picture.

snout   **tongue**   **wrinkles**

French bulldogs

German Shepherds

They become your friend.
They keep you safe.

Fetch the Answer

Q: Why do police use German shepherds?

A: These dogs are smart and easy to teach. They can sniff out danger and find missing people.

adult German shepherd

Huskies

They like the snow.

Thick fur keeps them warm.

adult huskies

Expert Fact

Huskies don't bark much.
But they do like to **howl**.

All the Puppies

They are adorable.
Thanks, puppies!

1.

2.

5.

6.

Expert Quiz

Do you know the names of these puppies? Then you are an expert! See if someone else can name them too!

3.

4.

7.

8.

Answers: 1. Poodle. 2. Retriever. 3. Huskies. 4. Terrier. 5. Pointer. 6. Bulldog. 7. Beagle. 8. German shepherd.

21

Expert Gear

Meet a dog groomer, a person who washes puppies and trims their fur. What does she need to keep puppies looking good?

She has a **comb**.

She has a **brush**.

She has **scissors**.

She has **hair clippers**.

Glossary

bark (BAHRK): to make the sudden, harsh sound of a dog.

howl (HOUL): to make a loud, long cry or sound.

shed (SHED): when bits of fur come off a dog or other animal.

webbed (WEBD): having a fold of skin that connects the toes.

Index

Names: Kelly, Erin Suzanne, 1965- author.
Title: Puppies/by Erin Kelly.
Description: New York: Children's Press, an imprint of Scholastic Inc., 2021. | Series: Be an expert! | Audience: Ages 3-5. | Audience: Grades K-1. | Summary: "Learn all about puppies with this exciting new book!"— Provided by publisher.
Identifiers: LCCN 2020031141 | ISBN 9780531136799 (library binding) | ISBN 9780531136805 (paperback)
Subjects: LCSH: Puppies—Juvenile literature. | CYAC: Dogs.
Classification: LCC SF426.5 .K45 2021 | DDC 636.7/07—dc23
LC record available at https://lccn.loc.gov/2020031141

Printed in Heshan, China 62

SCHOLASTIC, CHILDREN'S PRESS, BE AN EXPERT!™, and associated logos are trademarks and/or registered trademarks of Scholastic Inc.

1 2 3 4 5 6 7 8 9 10 R 30 29 28 27 26 25 24 23 22 21

Scholastic Inc., 557 Broadway, New York, NY 10012.

Art direction and design by THREE DOGS DESIGN LLC.

Photos ©: cover top and throughout: Heide Benser/Getty Images; cover center right: Juniors Bildarchiv GmbH/Alamy Images; cover bottom center: Mark Taylor/NPL/Minden Pictures; cover bottom right: Jane Burton/NPL/Minden Pictures; cover grass: almoond/Getty Images; 1 center: Mark Taylor/Minden Pictures; 1 center right: nycshooter/Getty Images; 2 bottom left: hartcreations/Getty Images; 3 top left: Mark Taylor/NPL/Minden Pictures; 3 center right: Mark Taylor/NPL/Minden Pictures; 7 sidebar bottom: Blue Jean Images/Alamy Images; 8-9 background: almoond/Getty Images; 11 butterflies: posteriori/Getty Images; 11 sidebar bottom: Jessica Lynn Culver/Getty Images; 12 center: 3bugsmom/Getty Images; 12 bottom: Jane Burton/NPL/Minden Pictures; 13 sidebar bottom: sturti/Getty Images; 13 center: Juniors Bildarchiv GmbH/Alamy Images; 13 bottom: Jane Burton/NPL/Minden Pictures; 14 center: Mark Taylor/NPL/Minden Pictures; 16-17 foreground: Liyan Liyan/EyeEm/Getty Images; 20 bottom right: Mark Taylor/NPL/Minden Pictures; 21 sidebar: hartcreations/Getty Images; 21 bottom left, bottom right: Mark Taylor/NPL/Minden Pictures; 22 center: Blue Jean Images/Alamy Images; 23 bottom: Photos by R A Kearton/Getty Images.

All other photos © Shutterstock.